I HOPE THIS MAKES YOU UNCOMFORTABLE

KAT SAVAGE

This is a work of fiction. Names, characters, places, and incidents either are the product of the author's imagination or are used fictitiously. Any resemblance to actual persons, living or dead, events, or locales is entirely coincidental.

Copyright © 2022 by Kat Savage
All rights reserved.

No part of this book may be reproduced or used in any manner without written permission of the copyright owner except for the use of quotations in a book review.

thekatsavage@gmail.com

Cover Design by Kat Savage
Edited by Christina Hart

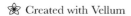 Created with Vellum

Also By Kat Savage

Poetry

Mad Woman

Let Me Count The Ways

Counting Backwards From Gone

I Hope This Makes You Uncomfortable

Letters From A Dead Girl

Novels

For Now

With This Lie

A Fighting Chance

One More Chance

Taking A Chance

Hawk

Will

Avery

Hanson

the way we carry pain

I CAN STILL HEAR IT,

the bellowing deep belly laugh

of my abuser

beating tirelessly against my ear drums,

startling me awake in the middle of the night

So I lie there

tracing my eyes over invisible shapes creating themselves

in the still and silent darkness swirling around me

I cannot remember the color of his eyes,

except on days when the sky turns

cold and dark and gray,

and a chill runs down my spine with an all-too-familiar

feeling that he is watching me even though

I haven't seen him,

not really, not in flesh and blood

Now he is only a phantom,

a ghostly apparition floating over me,

a balloon forever chained to my wrist

I carry him like this,

his heaviness, his breathing,

his unexplainable aftertaste

sitting on the back of my tongue

I draw salt circles around my body,

pray I can keep his memory out of this broken

but still holy place,

this body, my body

That's the way it is

Some days, I am all powerful,

protecting myself with incantations

and daring trespassers to enter if they dare

Other days, I am lighting candle vigils, mourning,

piling memories of my innocence

against a chain link fence

It is this, it will always be this

Back and forth,

my state of mind a pendulum,

a broken clock

Rewind, fast forward

Stop

Please stop

i hope this makes you uncomfortable

I HOPE this makes you uncomfortable,

I hope this crying out,

this confrontation of injustice

seeps into your marrow,

causes the tiny hairs on your neck

to stand in attention

I hope this makes you uncomfortable,

my voice raging onward, raging outward

from my frail frame

for a cause much bigger than myself,

bigger than all of us

I hope this makes you uncomfortable,

the way I look here,

invisible bruises in patchwork

over my skin,

bloodied lips

I am hemorrhaging,

I am in pieces

No means no

but the sinners are deaf

I hope this makes you uncomfortable

the way I am uncomfortable

every single day

do you feel it?

Do you feel it?

The unsettling ache inside your chest

when you try to breathe deeply in a world

so shallow we all split our heads open

on the bottom because you dive in, eyes closed, heart open
and disappointment begins to bleed from your wounds,

bone chips and dark debris floating in a cloud of self-hate
all around you

The chlorine stings your most sensitive parts,

and soon you won't even know

you hurt yourself because you died trying

. . .

You wake up in some other place,

in some other time, desperate and delusional

for a love so filthy you can't get clean

even when your shower is so hot

it turns your skin red as you lick away tears

rolling down your cheeks

You try to remember a time the love you had

yor yourself was enough and who stripped it away, left a dollar bill in the elastic of your panties, said they'd call you tomorrow

Do you feel it?

The glossing over, the jaded projection of your lack of affection falling over your life like a blanket of cigar smoke

Do you feel it?

The moment you shifted from naïve girl

to scorned woman

I bet your lips taste like venom now

I hope you kill them all

. . .

There are so many ways to die

i don't want to starve

HE ASKED me
if I've ever kissed the lips
of a man who didn't
ask me to apologize
for existing
I tell him no

he asks me if I want to
I tell him I'm afraid of what
that might taste like
he asks me why
I tell him that's the sort of thing
a woman like me will fall in love with
I tell him I don't want to starve myself

. . .

he shakes his head

I laugh

he undresses me against the wall
and pushes himself inside me
but we never kiss
I wonder what that means

I am only a ghost
and I watch him visit my grave

the personification of mental illness

THERE'S a bottle of Prozac in my bag
and I visit it every day,
though sometimes I forget.
Do you know what it's like to feel guilty
because you missed your medication?

Generalized anxiety disorder
makes my leg bounce
and my mind race.

Then I get a migraine,
and it crawls through my temples
and rests behind my eyes.

. . .

So I take a pill for that,
sometimes two or three.

I forgot to take my Prozac again.
Oh no, I'm going to get sad again.
My depression is in the corner
rubbing its hands together—
the boogeyman in my nightmares.

Just one more, it says.
Forget one more and I'll be there
to fall in the blackness with you.

It's 2PM so I take the pill,
the little green capsule
that looks so happy,
will make me happy.

Another migraine,
three more pills.

Better take my vitamins too,
drink some water.

It's probably dehydration.

Better not check my blood pressure.
My mother had a heart attack at 37.
That's only three years away,
my anxiety whispers.
Won't let me forget.

There are two types of people in this world:
the medicated
and the need to be medicated.
I don't know which is doing better
but if you give me a moment,
I'll let my depression tell you all about it.

a society like athena

NOTHING HAS CHANGED

In thousands of years,
nothing has changed
We want to believe it has,
we want to believe
we have evolved,
we have become better,
we have grown into
a more civilized people
We want to believe we are good
and kind and fair
But then I remember Medusa,
snakes for hair,

the monster they made her
I think about women today,
punished for being raped,
just like her
I just don't think they know yet
the monsters they are making

wielding weapons

My heart has always been a switchblade
but my hands have never learned
how to hold a weapon.

A dangerous combination for a lover.

I think it might've come in handy
on a few nights when my bed wasn't empty,
but I still felt the sting of unfiltered silence.
No one has a voice these days.

I heard a rumor going around about
what he's doing now but they meant
who he's doing now and

I hear she is a *peach*.
So sweet, so nourishing to his
hungry mouth.

And it makes sense to me,
that he would love a girl with soft skin.
A girl who feeds
rather than one who
cuts him,
who leaves his fingers
bleeding and reaching.

leave a light on

It's gonna hit you different,
the first time you see him smiling
and you're not the reason behind it

You're not gonna understand it yet,
how you're still neck deep in the ache
and he's floating on a foreign cloud nine

It's gonna be like standing in a room full of people laughing but no one told you the goddamn joke

The song playing in the background
is the one you showed him the day you met
and he wouldn't even know it without you

and you're wondering how he remembers

in parts, never mentions the whole,

has you realizing you're the punchline

It feels like a tragedy, something you see on

the morning news and the anchor mispronounces your name

You're forgotten in a pile of past lovers

you're thinking to yourself you don't understand how you're a drop in the ocean for him

But for you,

for you

He's the island you're shipwrecked on,

the place you can't escape and don't want to

Fast forward to next year, new year, new you

You haven't thought about him in so long until one night he crosses the road in front of you, a diamond on her hand glistens, reflects the red light

Suddenly you can't breathe and you don't want to because every time you inhale, you exhale his name

. . .

Still quick on your tongue, rubs against your teeth, is an open wound

He turns at the last moment,
sees you seeing him, nods, smiles fondly

You spend the rest of the night
wondering if you live inside his head
the way he lives inside yours

You hope with everything
you can turn the lights out soon

such a good liar

I SHOULD LIKE to go

to the tall green grass

and sit

and sigh

and feel something

beyond this cage

I have put myself in,

to feel free

of this brokenness

I carry

. . .

because I know nothing else,
because I believe I can be
nothing else

I am such a good liar

only,
I have been doing it so long,
I don't know which version of me is the lie

what is the cage?
what is freedom?

daddy issues

YOU CALL IT DADDY ISSUES.
I call it a fear of abandonment.
I don't know the shape of my father's face,
but I've been told I have his nose.

You call it daddy issues.
I call it the reason I assume everyone
will leave.

An entire generation of daughters,
abandoned by their fathers.
They were not men,
but we still wear their names
like a badge,

as if there is honor in doing so.

You call it daddy issues.
I call it the root of all my sad poems.

You slapped a label on it,
blamed the daughters.
You say I shouldn't
feel his absence,
but you make me carry it,
remind me each time
I love a man who doesn't love me.
You call it daddy issues.
I call it an identity crisis.

I'm the type of woman
who always stays,
always hopes if I love him
hard enough
he'll love me back.

You call it daddy issues.
I call it the reason I know no other way.

. . .

What does it really mean?

Hello.

I'm in pieces.

Please love me.

I want to feel warmth,

like the womb I cannot crawl back into.

impressively sad

BEFORE THE BRUISES,

before the deep purple-black blotches

turned awful yellow,

the regret marked all over

my once perfect skin

seeped deep down

into my internal organs,

my pigment was peach flesh,

sweet,

untainted

but even when they fade,

they leave something behind

something not to be named,

something unmistakably

impressive but sad

.

i do not fit

You have beautiful hands

A flick of your wrists and

they bow like a sickled moon,

empty and waiting

If I could draw them in all their perfection,

I could make you see

what I see,

what everyone sees

I knew if I tried hard enough,

I could fill that hungry curve with myself

That was my problem

I was always trying to bend

and fold and twist to fit into your

empty spaces so you could carry me—
you were always flattening your palms,
so I would spill out all over the night sky
Hungry, but not for me
Wanting, but not for me

mapping conversations

I COULD DECONSTRUCT

our last conversation,

break it down to basic parts,

underline the nouns,

highlight the adjectives,

branch the prepositional phrases,

but still

not understand

your curled lips,

ratcheted, wound tightly,

a key in the back of a doll,

and sometimes I am the doll

Your expensive words

cave in on your cheap message,

you've assembled this
backwards,
you've assembled this nothing
and yet,

you make leaving me
sound so beautiful,
not like an apology,
not like a goodbye,
you make leaving me
sound like forgiveness

loving liars

I LIKE you
and all the promises
you hold in your hands,
fold into my skin,
sew in deep
This is my error in judgment,
something you shouldn't
concern yourself with

I like the way your mouth moves
even when you are
whispering lies,
the great promise-breaker
that you are

I know no different,
because this is all I have
to show for my life,
all I have experienced
It is second nature for me
to love a liar

I am the patsy for your
self-destruction,
I am the collateral damage
for your apathy,
the human sacrifice always,
in so many ways

You will run as you always do
I will hide, take cover,
as I have learned to do,
instilled and beaten into me,
this is a way of life

deep inside

HOW MANY TIMES

does a person shed their skin

in a lifetime?

how many times

do they peel away layers

of themselves

hoping to be cleansed?

born again?

better than before?

when the greater fear is,

the dirt is somewhere

inside,

somewhere we cannot reach,

and no amount of scrubbing

will take it away

erase and rewind

IF I HAD KNOWN
you were leaving,
I'd have played us
in reverse,

rewound the clocks,
unbroken the promises,
unsmashed the photo frames,
moved back out,

all the way back to the beginning
when everything was new,
exciting,
when we were both filled with hope,

with courage,

with trying,

so when this ended
we found ourselves saying

Hello, it's so nice to meet you
Please come and sit with me
I cannot wait to kiss you
for the first time,
for the last time

begging

I'M JUST SITTING HERE

waiting for you

to read my mind,

I have left it unguarded,

here is the key

Read between

the lines of our texts,

where I know I left bread crumbs,

tiny hints for you to follow

all the way back to me,

understand

the things I want you to do

without having to tell you,
without having to beg
I covet your attention,
please give me your attention

I need you to understand me
even when I don't,
when I can't

selfish is as selfish does

I WANT to tell you

so many things,

things I think you should know,

deserve to know

I want to tell you

about all the ways

I will fail to love you

It would start small,

a forgotten call,

a missed note,

turn into poor excuses,

less sex, less affection,

flip the page to no sex,

rolling eyes,

utter disappointment

But I can't summon them

from my throat

and not warning you

will be my first betrayal

I am too selfish for this,

I have always been too selfish for this

poem #08

I feel so invisible

in all the wrong ways

My voice manifests

from this nothingness

Please,

pull me out of this

copper pieces

On quiet nights,

I can recall those tender moments

when we were in bed

and you leaned in

to whisper some beautiful something

(I never understood why they'd call them nothings)

against my ear,

I flutter,

I flush

Time passes

quietly,

flies under the radar,

I could hardly feel it,

and it twists your words into pennies,
cheap copper pieces
that I keep dropping into wishing wells,
into the open wound in my chest

You must have said goodbye
a dozen different ways
Here I am,
still closing my eyes
& hearing everything but what
you were actually saying

come morning

I AM the product
of too many unfinished kisses,
unhad conversations,
unwanted advances,
and not enough scenarios
in which you stay all night,
make coffee or breakfast,
or the bed

Which is to say,
I wish you were here
to kiss me in the morning,
to hold me tightly in protest of the sunlight,

run us both a shower

Which is to say,
this is no longer enough,
has never been enough

sleeping alone

WE PREPARE FOR BED,

our night routine as soft

as any other

I take the dogs out

one last time,

you pick a movie,

background noise,

the lullaby we fall

asleep to

we crawl

beneath the blankets,

no goodnight passes

our lips,

no kiss to end the day,

a valley of silence

between us

I turn to my side,

you to yours,

the space growing bigger

I fall asleep

each night

wondering

how many more

I will fall asleep

alone

invisible walls

You fall asleep—

not next to me

but not too far away, either.

If I reach, stretch far enough,

I could run my fingers over the

bridge of your nose,

listen for the small moan

to escape you at my touch—

the one my ears beg for.

The warmth of your skin

will remind me

how much I miss it,

how I long for it.

So close,

but the bitter built

a wall between us—

invisible

and strong.

Stronger than me.

empty line

I HAVE FORGOTTEN

what you look like

first thing in the morning

It was the first thing to slip from my mind

when you packed up, pulled out

You took care in not leaving behind hints of yourself,

no toothbrush, no shadow trapped in a drawer

I cannot remember

the color of your sleepy eyes

or how your soft, warm skin

felt against mine

I do not smell you on my

pillow anymore,

and I keep piles of folded clothes

on your side to keep balance

Just like that,

not a slow fade,

but a dropped call,

I am still on the other line,

hello? hello? hello?

into the silence,

gone

unsee the pain

THERE'S a chunk of foam missing
from the armrest of the chair I sit in at work.
It was already gone when I arrived,
a hand-me-down chair
with a hand-me-down story.

Did anxious fingers dig a hole for distraction?
Did worried hands rub it into submission?
I'll never know.

Sometimes I think about running my car
off the road, into a ditch,
making deep long tire marks
in the earth—

gashed open like cuts,

like wounds that will never heal.

I think about who might come along and

wonder where they came from—

if it was an accident,

if it was a suicide attempt.

The world is full of missing chunks

and tire mark wounds.

If you open your eyes wide enough,

for long enough,

you won't be able to unsee them.

regret me

I AM WAITING for you to regret me

just like the rest of them,

just like always

Throw me back

I am not a keeper

I am never anyone's first choice,

only a consolation prize,

the leftovers,

never *the* woman

only the *other* woman

I am waiting for you to wake up

and miss what was before me,

to miss what could have been

with someone else,

someone better

panic attack

AT LEAST,

at least tell me you miss me

so I can still this silent panic attack,

this rumbling,

this crumbling

warring under my skin

as I sink into the center of this empty bed

and try to mold you from my pillows,

try to find your ghost

in these empty sheets

But I can never get your face right,

or feel your heartbeat

beneath the pillowcase

Your warmth is gone from this place,

this place that was ours

If you were here,

I'd kiss each of your fingertips,

fold myself into your ribs,

and ask you to leave your smile behind

if you must go again,

if you must go again

a vulture, a boy

Looking back, I can see it,

I can see the trail of

jet black feathers all around

You were hungry,

a vulture looking to pick me off,

looking to make a meal of me

I was young and didn't know

all the ways you

(and the world)

would eventually break me

Four months later,

you broke my hymen

while I was bent over a rock

in the woods behind my house
It was nothing like they said it would be
I went inside, threw away my panties,
and bled, and cried
(so romantic)

When I stopped,
I looked in the mirror
and tried to find the woman
inside my fifteen-year-old skin
She was not there

A year later,
you left a bruise on my arm
and I lied to my parents
and told them I ran into a door,
and I was too young to be there, like that

When you left me,
you convinced me it was my fault,
that I wasn't good enough,
that I didn't fulfill you

. . .

I cannot get that back

I cannot let that go

It took me two years to realize

I shouldn't miss you

You did that,

that is your fault

I wonder what she would have been like,

the girl who didn't meet the vulture,

the girl I could have been

if I had been able to hold onto

my innocence

just a little

while

longer

hollow imposter

I DIDN'T KNOW

the absence of touch,

of attention

could leave such

a heavy

imprint

could

mark me up

in such a way

I stop

desiring it,

stop remembering

what it's like

the brush of

a fingertip

across my jawline,

the palm of a hand

aching with desire to be

wetted with a kiss,

retraining my wrist

to arch

what does love

feel like

without touch?

like this,

like nothing at all

a hollow imposter

suicidal arsonist

I FEEL the twist of a dagger

in my side

and

I am reminded

just how far I have fallen,

just how much I have not done

I cannot get up this mountain,

cannot see the other side

I knew myself better

once upon a time,

a phrase not always used

for a happy ending

. . .

I am the one holding the dagger
Don't tell

Do you know what it's like
to watch your world burn
and realize too late
that you're the one
holding the match?

this life is made up of ugly things

I AM SPLITTING myself open
in a world that will never
understand me
but I split myself open
to be understood
Maybe I haven't exposed enough
Not yet

I look around and feel
more than I should,
more than I can handle
and I weep
and worry
until my knuckles are white,

nail beds chewed and bleeding,
hair in the drain

This blade wasn't always dull,
this armor not always in need
of mending
I've been at war too long
with enemies I can't see
who know me better than I know me

The truth is I am both
the blade
and the enemy

I am frozen in this place,
watching it come undone around me,
feeling it come undone within me,
hoping for better,
preparing for worse,
knowing neither matters
I swallow hard
on these pills,
these realizations

I pray harder

to a god

who might've forgotten me

because I have forgotten him,

to give me what I need

to defeat this

the masks we wear

SADNESS IS a disease

festering underneath my fingernails,

eroding my liver,

breaking me down

bit by bit

and I don't want to be cured,

I can't be cured

(nothing would remain)

It's chronic,

like so many things we label a choice

(no one would choose to be sad)

I hope he fucks me until I forget

(or maybe they would)

. . .

Just for tonight,

I don't want to have to remember

which person I am

and which person I pretend to be

(maybe I would)

the art of aching, part one

It's simple really,

the art of aching,

ingrained in me,

a muscle memory

I have retained

the ache is

in my skin,

behind my eyes,

it flicks from my tongue

in every word I speak

when I kiss lovers,

I leave some of it with them

. . .

you must wear it

as easily as a lazy smile,

a Mona Lisa smirk

drape it 'round your shoulders

like an expensive fur,

like a luxury lipstick

you must own it,

the ache,

hold it in the palm of your hand,

never let it go,

it belongs to you now,

and you to it

one day you will ask yourself

what you would be without it

the answer is nothing

I am nothing without the ache

a proud woman never begs

You are not particularly mean,

not on purpose,

it is just your nature

But you are not particularly kind either,

kindness takes real effort on your part

I don't know if you can see me,

silently begging for your attention,

hoping to be noticed

I want to say something,

to ask,

to plead

But I am both too proud

and too worried
to break in that particular way
and that's saying something
because I break in so many ways
over and over again
all the damn time

I sigh,
I retreat

I hope you will read my mind,
my body language

I need you
to see me

unborn

I AM WATCHING you fall out of love with me.

Your eyes are fading—

the sparkle dim.

They no longer glisten for me.

Your body recoils from me,

in slow motion.

We are in reverse,

a death sentence,

the undoing slow,

like being unborn.

I can't pull anything from you—

not a laugh, not a smile.
You kiss me,
but I don't feel it.
And where is your tongue?

I haven't seen your passion.
I don't know where you hid it.
I already checked your wallet.

If you leave me,
I'll feel it.
Like a wave crashing at my ankles,
like a rubber bullet to a chest plate.

And then I'll mourn,
and then I'll get over it.

a tragedy in four acts

If I could write you into a tragedy,

it would feel something like this

Act One

He will kiss the palm of your hand

every day

and you will feel it everywhere,

make you feel like you are the only one

for the first time in your life

You will feel whole

for the first time in your life

Act Two

He will be kissing her, too

and you will know only when it's too late,

after the damage has been done

You will find out you were the one

tucked away like a gentle secret,

the other one,

the one he runs to

only when he wants to

Act Three

You will forgive him because

that is what love does

and despite all of it,

you do love him

and you have known this kind of disappointment

all your life

so it's okay

Act Four

You will never forgive yourself

even though you didn't do anything wrong,

even though all you did

was give your heart away,

because you should have known better,

because hating your own skin is so much easier,

because everything that happens to you is your fault

(because these are the biggest lies we tell ourselves)

The End

you think you know

THERE IS ONLY POISON HERE,

in my veins,

on my hands,

dripping from my lips

and your smug smile

will be the death of you

I will ruin you,

ruin the idea of me for you,

ruin what you think you want

because it is not me

even though you're convinced otherwise

You will never know what hit you,

a sucker punch to your belief system,

I will stand over you,

laughing,

asking you to tell me again

how you will wreck me

the way lies take from you

They tell me I won't feel this
after a little time has gone by,
after a little space is between me
and this unpleasant thing,
this terrible thing,
this betrayal of my trust

They tell me I won't see the scar
after a little while,
after I've healed,
that I won't rub the tip of my finger
over the jagged line running
across my shoulder blade

. . .

They tell me how easy it will be

this time next year to believe again

in love and people,

to believe again

in myself, in my worth

But they are liars,

just like you,

and each time

you take something from me,

something I can't get back,

I am never the same again

measuring time

I MET you three years after she died

and two years before I figured out

who you really were

Measurements of time

are funny sometimes,

we measure by milestones and events

I couldn't tell you

the date on the calendar

or what the clock on the wall read,

but I remember

the sun setting on our faces

and the way the water moved

over the rocks

just a few feet away from us

You got a peanut butter milkshake that day

but I've never seen you order one since,

and maybe you use that as a measurement yourself

Sometimes I wonder what you were like

before we met and

in my mind you were different then,

kinder eyes,

maybe a brighter smile

I cannot help but think

I am the one who dulled you down,

I am the one who took away your light

Maybe finding me

was not what you were meant to do,

maybe this is not where you were meant to be

i will not shut up

Do you know what it's like

to have to look someone in the eyes

and defend your truth?

Do you know what it's like

to have strangers run their eyes

over your body and dismiss

what it has endured?

To them,

I look whole

and so

they assume

it's not that bad,

that I can't possibly

be carrying it around still

They don't understand

the weight of fingerprints,

the discomfort of what the showers

will not wash away

They want to tell me how I should feel,

they want to downplay my pain,

fit it into a shoebox and make me

shove it under my bed,

the same bed where I toss and turn

and wake up in the middle of the night

in a cold sweat because I can still feel him

in places I didn't give him permission to be

They want to shut me up,

cut my tongue out,

make me mute,

so I can't say the words,

the ones that give them nightmares

Theirs, works of fiction

Mine, memories on repeat

I will say it again and again,

the headlines that make you cringe

are my life

I will not go quietly

I will not shut up

you, the political platform

I AM nothing more than a mechanism,

a useful anecdote at parties,

a political talking point

as both a woman

and a victim,

excuse me, survivor

They will talk until they're blue in the face,

blowing hot air from their round and puffed cheeks,

asking for my vote,

my support,

promising, promising

for better policies,

more justice,

less blame,

a better world

with better people

But they do not control

the people, the monsters

They cannot promise you a thing

they cannot control

Remember that

when they start spitting speeches

at podiums

You are a platform they do not understand

and they cannot promise you a thing

they cannot control

crucifixion

I BROKE myself
Be careful where you step—
there are pieces of me everywhere

I am the man hanging on the cross
and I am the cross
crucified myself without hesitation

what does regret feel like?
A nail driven through the palm of my hand

The bruises you left are a crown of thorns

Oh, how I mourn

expectations

I HOISTED you up

on top of a shiny white pedestal

against your will

and let my disappointment

in you

fester inside my rib cage

and then I blamed you for it

This is how it goes,

this is always how it goes

This is how it unravels,

when expectations and realities

are not the same

It wasn't your fault

that you weren't the way

I wanted you to be

It wasn't your fault

that I pretended you were

i know a girl

I KNOW a girl who is still in love
with her abuser
Scratch that
I know a girl who is still in love
with the boy who raped her,
the boy who forced himself
inside her
against her will,
without her permission,
words would not stop him
I know a girl who is still in love
with the boy who ruined her,
who betrayed her trust,
broke her down,

treated her as less important
than she is
I know a girl who is still in love
with the boy who reduced her
to broken,
damaged her inside and out,
made her a thing for his use,
made her into someone

who doesn't understand her worth

I KNOW a girl who is still in love

with the boy who raped her

because her whole life was violence,

her whole life was mistreatment,

her whole life the people closest to her

made her believe she was less than she was

She is everything

but doesn't see it,

deserving of love

but doesn't feel it,

human, inherently valuable

but has never been shown

this kindness

If this isn't trauma,

a thing to be untaught,

if this isn't the saddest

you could feel

for a girl who needs a loving hand,

I don't know what is

coming out

My first kiss was a girl in fourth grade,
my best friend
She had red hair and freckles
and I had no idea
when she dared me to kiss her
it was because she liked me,
like,
like liked me
the way I understood only
boys and girls liked each other at the time
Since finding out about her struggle
with her own sexuality,
I've often wondered
what it must have been like for her,

a girl,

lost and confused inside her own body,

not understanding why she doesn't want

to put little boys' names inside her heart scribbles

and why her heart flutters every time

she is with her best friend

who is a girl just like her

Imagine, your womanhood not yet bloomed

and already your body feels wrong

because you know no better,

because you do not know you can love anyone

Imagine, if you will, growing into your body,

its strange cravings you can't share with anyone

because you fear

there is something wrong with you,

fear what this means

I grew up liking both boys and girls

before I knew there was a word for it

My coming out was less a conversation

and more a passing comment,

no shock on my parents' faces,

no shame, no questions

I wonder about the children

who don't have it so easy,
who can't speak their truth
for fear of their condemnation
I wonder about my old friend,
I hope she is happy
I hope she is loved

the pursuit of perfection

EVERYBODY KNOWS

that one mistake

carries the same weight

as seven right things

So when I

cook a delicious dinner

and go to the grocery

and pick up your favorite snacks

and lay out your work boots

and fold your laundry

and give you the best blow job

and feed the dog

but forget to put your phone on the charger

all on a typical Tuesday,

I have failed you
and will try again Wednesday
to not fuck up,
to not be so *me*
This is a behavior engrained in me
long before you
so it's not your fault
but I can hear the ring of
disappointment in your words
as they fall out of your mouth
and I know you're thinking it,
what a fuck up
The strive for perfection
started with my third-grade report card,
I was not good at science
and if it's not an A, it's not good enough
It followed me through high school,
why take regular classes when you can take AP?
In college,
I wasn't living up to my potential because
I was not valedictorian
but did I mention my dad shamed me
for having a brownie at my graduation dinner

because I had mentioned gaining weight?

Perfection and the pursuit of it

are devices meant to kill your spirit

and to my disbelief,

they took mine, too

insecurities

I can't understand things like

love

or

mercy

when I watch him text her,

tuck his phone away

I hate myself for

every moment I spend

in jealousy,

wonder how long I have been

this woman,

always so needy

I want to reach out

and touch his jawline,

feel the rough of his beard

beneath my hand

I want to kiss him,

lips parted,

tongue swollen against

the roof of my mouth

But I am afraid

of acceptance,

of rejection,

of the possibility

that both can exist

at the same time

I want to ask him

if he loves me for the sixth time today

but I know he will roll his eyes at me,

sigh, exhale,

tell me of course he does

I'm not sure if I'm afraid he's lying

or afraid he's telling the truth

Either way I don't want to read

the disappointment in my question

across his face

He doesn't understand things like

insecurities

or

reassurances

when I need them,

when I am begging for them

I wonder how long we will dance like this

the kill

I NEVER SAW it coming

It unraveled right in front of me

and I was blind to it,

blind to the truth

I am a lion

watching another lion

eat my prey

She came in,

teeth exposed,

has him by the neck,

isn't giving him back

And god how I want him back

He is a great wildebeest,

wounded and bleeding,

the light is leaving his eyes,

he is almost all gone

I could have saved him

but I didn't want to

This is my truth

I am too consuming,

I drive them all away

and into the mouths of others

and they'll happily die by another's hand

but never mine

I am never worth the agony of death,

I am never enough to surrender to

I watch them,

and they seem happy,

their eyes glossing over,

oblivious,

happy

I watch them,

as they are cut down,

watered down

into something else

And I could've stopped it,

I could've saved them

If only they wanted to be saved

it feels like suffocating

My breath catches
each time I feel hands
ripping my panties down over my thighs,
I panic and grab at them
only to discover they are still in place
I've heard of ghost limbs
but I didn't know
there were ghost moments
My lungs still with every
relived memory,
every nightmare come to life
My head is under water,
eyes closed,
I can feel the tiny bubbles

tickle my skin

as they escape to the surface

This is the only place

I cannot feel him

Sometimes I bury my face

deep into my pillow

just to get away

If I am focused on my breathing

or lack thereof,

I don't feel anything else

The only way to escape one thing

is to give all of them up

Feel nothing so I can't feel the bad,

feel everything and wish I could

escape it all

If I can find the place

just before I can't breathe, and stay there,

feel nothing,

maybe I would be okay

no returns, no exchanges

I HAVE WHISPERED my secrets into
the roots of this city—
into the brick walls of bar alleys,
into the cool leather
of taxi cab backseats,
and into the hearts of
a few lonely men
wandering the streets
who weren't quite as lonely
after we lied together.

But it's all bullshit.
An illusion.

. . .

And I've been trading secrets
like baseball cards
trying to get the parts of me back
I lost long ago.
What no one tells you,
is *once gone, always gone.*

*And you have to live a life
less whole to pay for
having things you don't deserve.*

the problem with god

GET on your knees

repent

apologize for all the things you did not do

for yourself

in the name of love

get on your knees

put him in your mouth

repent

he's going to take your name in vain

looking up at him from the floor

you're a god

he's a god

tell him the sins you want to commit with your body

the problem with god

is you can make one out of anything

out of anyone

get on your knees

pray

repent

gag order

I BET if I licked your palm
I would taste all the things
you stopped me from saying,
as if your hand had covered my mouth,
as if my courage had been embedded
beneath your fingernails,
as if there were a white-chalk outline
of me somewhere between
the alley behind the bar
and your 400-count Egyptian cotton sheets.
I bet if I looked hard enough
I'd find myself somewhere between
I don't want to

and

you didn't ruin me.

your mess to clean up

I swept my pain under the rug,
let the earth quake and crumble
beneath us.
Waited for you to save me,
save us.
You're the great earth shaker,
after all.
You're the mess maker,
it would seem.

Why didn't you save us?
There's a
drip drip drip
from the faucet

in our kitchen.

There's no paint on the walls;
the floors are only half-done.
You're letting our house fall apart
all around us,
letting the walls collect cobwebs,
all the while singing to me, that
everything is gonna be all right,
with a can of gasoline in one hand,
a match in the other.
You can't put ashes back together,
and there is no phoenix rising.

In this story,
there's no happily ever after,
only the promise
that soon,
it won't hurt anymore.

time & death

I TIP the hourglass

onto its side,

the sand not moving,

not traveling from one end

to the other.

I wish time was really like this.

I wish I could turn back several clocks.

I wish I didn't cry every time

I listened to that song

about sleeping forever.

Death has taught me many things.

Like how to suppress my emotions,

how to compartmentalize,

to let go in the car on the ride home

while the song about

overdosing plays loud,

so I don't fall apart when I get home.

Like how to smile for the kids

when I want to scream.

Death has taught me many things.

Like how to look at a simple T-shirt

and choke back a sob,

smell a familiar perfume,

choke back a laugh about that time

you wanted to adopt all the cats,

how being a mother is wonderful,

how you never stop needing your mother.

Death has taught me many things.

Like how to be mad and sad

at the exact same time.

you

Contrary to popular belief,

sadness seeps from me every single time

I think of you.

Sometimes I imagine

wrapping my hand

around your throat one more time.

You—

the nameless man from my past,

the faceless one in my dreams.

You—

the amalgamation,

the summation,

the combination

of all the men

who have choked on words like

I love you,

this isn't working,

I don't want to stay,

I need you,

you're not the one,

please don't go.

looking for god

I LOOKED in all the wrong places for god

wanted to feel him

but didn't feel him

in the weight of a stranger

pressed against the inside of my thighs

pressed my hands together

like a good girl

like a smart girl

asking for a ticket to anywhere except looking at herself in the mirror

hoped desperately god would find me

take care of me

. . .

didn't feel him in the weight of the man who pressed me deep into the mattress

didn't feel him when my lungs burned

suffocation can be so intoxicating

wash it down with forgiveness
for yourself

watch
as everything and nothing
makes you feel better

the art of aching, part two

I THINK it's in the way we hold ourselves together, the way we try so hard

not to fall apart

It's admirable, even if we're always

leaving morsels of ourselves behind,

even if the world cannot see our *try*

The ache causes a vibration in our chest

we're all sure will rip us apart someday,

but we're in denial about when and where

It'll be when you least expect it—

holding his hand on the couch,

out for drinks with that one girl,

on the way home from the concert

You won't feel it all at once

and then you will

I don't know why it's this way,

why it's like falling asleep

You have to hold it so tight to your breast plate that it can't escape your grip

You have to tame the ache,

create from it something worth passing on,

make with it an olive branch

to give the monster that sleeps next to you

If you give it something to chew on,

you might survive another night

You must use it as a shield,

to keep the rest at bay

it's just a manic episode

Nothing to be concerned about,
I'll return to regularly scheduled programming shortly

In the meantime,
please enjoy this montage
of all the ways I've fucked up
and doused myself in regret

Does this poem feel like
self-loathing to anyone else?
Just me?

I'll get over myself soon, I think
But probably not

doom

Again I come

again and again

flapping my pathetic wings

Over and over

the destination is

always the same—

to my doom

The flickering flams licks,

bites

. . .

My delicate wing,

my delicate wrist

my doom—

always you

some other place & time

In another life,
I never left

We're both sitting at our typewriters,
you're sipping something
from a local brewery,
I'm nursing a glass of sweet red

The room is filled with Hozier on vinyl,
our puppy sitting at our feet

You show me the poem about the girl
in Kentucky who stole your heart

. . .

I show you the one about

the poet

who tames me

We crawl into the bed we share,

you press your lips against mine,

the most perfect kiss that ever existed

You tell me I taste sweet, wine stained,

I inhale you

We fall asleep and I have a nightmare about

a life without you

So yeah

I guess you could say I still think about you

salt circles

THIS IS ALL JUST a defense mechanism,
a spotlight on my ugly thoughts,
drawn around me like salt circles

I say,
look here
see my pain
feel it sting your eyes
let it fill you with misery
because you're a slut for company

If I weaponize my depression,
my sadness,
all the trauma

. . .

you can't use it against me

It is a shield and a sword

a ramp and a ditch

a cure

and a poison

poets kill themselves because

THEY HAVE no value unless they're sad

no worth unless they're drowning

mean nothing if they don't share everything

just not the happiness

never the happiness

because no one can relate

hiss & moan

LIKE A TONGUE-TIED black snake

fattened from a meal,

I hiss for you

to return to me,

slip yourself back on

like my shedding skin

like a sex worker on her knees

trying to get milk for the kid's cereal

in the morning,

I moan for you

to love me,

turn your heart back on

like my coffee maker in the morning

as foreign as a pale pink balloon

I THINK a lot about suicide

clarification

I don't think about committing suicide

I think about it in general terms,

the idea of it,

about how depressed I've been,

how none of it drove me to plan mine

how lucky I've been,

to have been to inches to the right

of that particular bullet

an internet counselor asked me

if I ever felt like hurting myself
seven times in a forty-five minute chat
and after I said no each time
diagnosed me with bipolar disorder

I decided he was completely full of shit
I don't know if that's self-preservation of logic

the point is,
my depression is not a death wish

it's a cinder block tied to my ankle
mafia style, my nose barely above the water line,
teasing me
the point is,
my depression is dreaming about
my mother's dead body falling over me
and I can't get up

it's not a hand gun
not a grenade
not a bottle of pills
it's the lump in my throat,

the ache in my legs,

the thunder in my chest,

the panic I feel

when I close my eyes and pray

it will never grow bigger than me

for a moment

I wonder who I would be without it,

as if I were as light

as a pale pink balloon

floating toward the heavens

imagine my disdain

how to leave

I DON'T KNOW if there's a right way
to leave
except to say
if you're going to do it,
don't wait around for nothing to change

don't sink your claws into anything
as you're walking out

make no ruckus

leave gently
quietly
calmly

. . .

slip away so the person you left

on the welcome mat

with a hand outstretched

begging for your return

cannot hear the echo

of your noise from

the empty places

in your once shared home

and the empty spaces

in their once open heart

social media is my own personal vault of masochism

You are standing on a beach somewhere in central America,

shirtless, your arm around her

Next photo

You are both waist deep in crystalline water,

smiling

Next photo

There is a diamond shining in the sunlight,

resting boldly on her left ring finger

I shut my facebook app and recall last year

when you told me you didn't think you were

the marrying type,

didn't think you were the commitment type

What you meant was

you weren't the committing to me

type

I get it now

It took me three days to delete you

It took me three days to get the February

our of my bones

I hate that I still think you are beautiful

and I hope she sees it

i don't even know anymore

I'VE HURT as many as
have hurt me

My hands are wounded,
and my hands are explosive

My heart is at war with me heart

I mean,
I am at war with my heart

Please,
cute me first,

make me bleed first

So at least then I can write about it

And you
You will live in the forevers of ink
and scar tissue

nothing inside

It's been

thirty minutes

and six hours

and four days

since I saw you last,

since I heard your voice last

And there's this silence here

in this void,

a space so silent

it's like you never occupied it

This is the reason people stop listening to music

. . .

Because when it's gone,

there is an emptiness in the air,

and in your skin

and in the place inside where you put your happiness

I cup my hand around my ear,

place it against your chest

Nothing

If conch shells hold oceans,

I could press my ear to you

and hear all the stillness of graveyards

this missing you

AT NIGHT,
I curl myself into the
moon shaped nest of pillows—
my spine half feline—
and let the longing for you
I've fought back all day
consume me
the way your body would
if you were here

This missing you
feels so much like
drowning
& so much like

a life jacket

at the exact same time

that I don't know

if I want to be rescued

(please rescue me)

every goodbye

I CARRY every goodbye
anyone has ever whispered to me
in a sacred space just under the edge
of my left ribcage

Some have said it
like a prayer,
others like a sigh of relief

A couple even made it sounds
like "I love you"
because they're good liars
& I'm glad I never
took them for their word

. . .

Goodbye is a tired thing,

a broken thing

Goodbye means nothing

& everything you want it to

Goodbye is a shadow

you hope you can sew back on

with a needle & thread

poison

Loving you is a vice I can't give up.
You are the poison in my veins,
the addiction I can't shake.

I surrender to you in ways
I didn't even know I could,
ways I never knew existed.

When you leave,
I will die whispering your name
into the darkness covering me.

bait

I THINK I've started to like the way
disappointment tastes on my tongue
when I ask you where you've been
and you make a martyr of me
one more time

I give you these moments
hoping your guilt will
force the truth out of you,
hoping you'll set us both free
but you never bite

And so I go on chasing your secrets,

swallowing your deceits,

and missing us

masochist or not

I TRADE nights at home

in the comfort

of his arms for things

like too many

happy hour specials

& hotel rooms

that charge by the hour

I'd like to say I spend

my days picking the

regret from my teeth

but it is absent from me

And when he rolls away from me

on the nights I do make my way home,

I don't reach for him

because I don't deserve him

& I go on punishing both of us

for my inability to let him

love me

starting over

I BOUGHT new bed sheets but kept
the old comforter

I sit quietly on my new couch, alone

There is a TV dinner in the microwave
and two empty bottles in the garbage

This new apartment doesn't smell like anything
and so it doesn't feel like home
so I burn candles to mask its blank slate scent

Your text message asks me how I am
and I've never been good at lying so

the bubble back is blank

and I hope you're anticipating a response

but you'll never get it

Silence is the only lie I can manage

You'll never know how this starting over numbs me

so far away

I LIE AWAKE some nights
wondering exactly how far away
you are from me
at that exact moment

On a good night,
I'll remember you are in the same city
On a bad night,
I don't remember where I am
and get the overwhelming feeling
you are so much further

Every now and then,

you are only on the other side

of my bed and still,

you cannot feel me

reaching out to you

The men before you

DID brutal things to my body.
And you made love to me five times
before I could convince you
to apply a little pressure to my neck.
And you were so sad
that I needed this to get off.
I am sorry for being what they made me.
I am sorry I do not understand your soft touch.
I am sorry my body is too much wreckage
and not enough flesh.

If I stand on the corner of

Broadway and Vine

I can see the benches in front of

the fountain where we sat.

I don't know how many nights

we ended up there but it feels

like too many and not enough

if I'm being honest.

You always sat back, smiling

that sly smile,

that I-want-to-kiss-you-but-not-here

smile.

. . .

I thought that smile was a good thing,
I thought it meant something
beautiful but all it really means
is there are too many people around
and it will mean too much
and feel too much like something
when you want it to be nothing.

"Tell me a secret" you said.

"I don't have anymore" I lied.

I never learned how to be single.

I went from LAX to the streets of
Charlotte, never by myself
but always abandoned.

Perhaps I didn't know myself
enough to know what would
make me feel more complete,
perhaps I didn't want to know.

What I do know is that
if they love me too much,
I will want to leave.
And if they don't love me enough,
I will want to stay.

. . .

If I close my eyes on

any sidewalk,

I can hear two things—

my own heart beating

& the whirring of a thousand

people passing by

whose hearts have been

broken just like mine.

They're secrets are here, too.

About the Author

Kat Savage resides in Louisville, Kentucky with her three beautiful children, her hunky spouse, and three spoiled ass dogs. She secretly has hopes of getting chickens one day.

She was driven to write out of a need for distraction and self-preservation after the death of her sister in 2013. Since then, it's snowballed into a full blown passion she can't escape. Even on the toughest days, she wouldn't want to. Her unique brand of storytelling ranges from tragic poetry to swoony rom coms and even a little darkness. She uses her real life experiences to fuel every word she puts on paper. She's published several collections of poetry and multiple novels.

Savage is a natural storyteller, getting better with each book. She tries to give the characters in her novels depth, whether they're serious or comical. Savage builds them in layers with the hope that you see a little of yourself in some of them.

About the Author

Kat Savage resides in Louisville, Kentucky with her three beautiful children, her hunky spouse, and three spoiled ass dogs. She secretly has hopes of getting chickens one day.

She was driven to write out of a need for distraction and self-preservation after the death of her sister in 2013. Since then, it's snowballed into a full blown passion she can't escape. Even on the toughest days, she wouldn't want to. Her unique brand of storytelling ranges from tragic poetry to swoony rom coms and even a little darkness. She uses her real life experiences to fuel every word she puts on paper. She's published several collections of poetry and multiple novels.

Savage is a natural storyteller, getting better with each book. She tries to give the characters in her novels depth, whether they're serious or comical. Savage builds them in layers with the hope that you see a little of yourself in some of them.

Made in the USA
Las Vegas, NV
24 October 2022